Wheels

Rob Sved

Contents

OXFORD
UNIVERSITY PRESS

UNIVERSITY PRESS

Great Clarendon Street, Oxford, OX2 6DP, United Kingdom

Oxford University Press is a department of the University of Oxford. It furthers the University's objective of excellence in research, scholarship, and education by publishing worldwide. Oxford is a registered trade mark of Oxford University Press in the UK and in certain other countries

© Oxford University Press 2012

The moral rights of the author have been asserted

First published in 2012

2016 2015 2014 2013 2012

10 9 8 7 6 5 4 3

No unauthorized photocopying

All rights reserved. No part of this publication may be reproduced, stored in a retrieval system, or transmitted, in any form or by any means, without the prior permission in writing of Oxford University Press, or as expressly permitted by law, by licence or under terms agreed with the appropriate reprographics rights organization. Enquiries concerning reproduction outside the scope of the above should be sent to the ELT Rights Department, Oxford University Press, at the address above

You must not circulate this work in any other form and you must impose this same condition on any acquirer

Links to third party websites are provided by Oxford in good faith and for information only. Oxford disclaims any responsibility for the materials contained in any third party website referenced in this work

ISBN: 978 0 19 464631 4

An Audio CD Pack containing this book and a CD is also available, ISBN 978 0 19 464641 3

The CD has a choice of American and British English recordings of the complete text.

An accompanying Activity Book is also available, ISBN 978 0 19 464652 9

Printed in China

This book is printed on paper from certified and well-managed sources.

ACKNOWLEDGEMENTS

Illustrations by: Kelly Kennedy pp.9, 13, 19; Alan Rowe pp.20, 21, 22, 23, 24, 26, 27, 30, 31.

The Publishers would also like to thank the following for their kind permission to reproduce photographs and other copyright material: Alamy pp.3 (bike wheels/Carlos Voss), 5 (bus/Mo Peerbacus, rollerskaters/MARKA), 15 (combine harvester/John McKenna); Corbis pp.6 (stroller/Corey Rich/Aurora Photos); Getty Images p.3 (train wheels/Panoramic Images, car wheels/Matthew Ward/Dorling Kindersley), 4 (Bob Langrish/Dorling Kindersley), 7 (wheelchair race/Jan Kruger/Getty Images Sport), 8 (cycle race/Sajjad Hussain/Stringer), 10 (Matthew Ward/Dorling Kindersley), 11 (plane/train/Panoramic Images), 13 (child on toy/Rune Johansen/Photolibrary), 14 (Chris Cheadle/Stone), 15 (pizza cutter/Lew Robertson/Photographer's Choice), 17 (rolling pin/Oleksly Maksymenko/All Canada Photos, paint roller/Steven Puetzer/Riser), 19 (Oliver Cleve/Photographer's Choice); Oxford University Press pp.3 (yo-yos), 6 (shopping trolley), 8 (woman cyclist), 9, 12, 13 (merry-go-round), 16 (alarm clock and x-ray of clock), 18; Rex Features p.7 (man in wheelchair/Sipa Press).

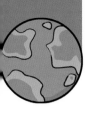 # Introduction

We use wheels every day. All wheels are round, but some wheels are big and some wheels are little. Wheels can do many things.

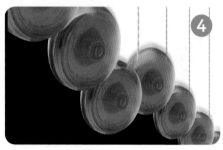

Where are these wheels?
Where can you see other wheels?

 Now read and discover more about wheels!

1 What Are Wheels?

Wheels are machines. Wheels are round and they turn. People use wheels to do many things.

People use wheels to carry things. This wheelbarrow has one wheel at the front. The girl walks and the wheel turns.

A Wheelbarrow

People use wheels to move. This school bus has four big wheels. It carries lots of people.

Wheels are fun, too. Look at these roller skates. A roller skate has four little wheels. With roller skates, people can move fast.

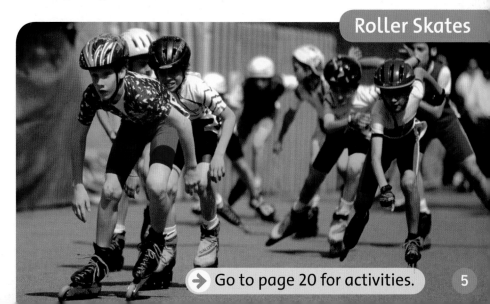

Go to page 20 for activities.

Carts and Chairs

In a store, people use a shopping cart to carry many things. The cart has little wheels. People can push and pull the cart.

A stroller has wheels, too. People push the strollers and babies can sleep in them.

A Shopping Cart

A Stroller

Some people can't walk. They use wheelchairs to move. They push the big wheels with their hands.

A Wheelchair

Discover!

People use wheelchairs in sports. These people are in a long race. They can go 42 kilometers in two hours!

→ Go to page 21 for activities.

3 Bicycles

helmet

Do you have a bicycle? Bicycles have two wheels. You use your legs to turn the wheels. You wear a helmet to protect your head.

Some bicycles can go very fast. These people are in a race.

A Race

metal wheel

pump

rubber tire

Look at this bicycle wheel. It's a metal wheel with a rubber tire. The tire helps the wheel to turn on bumpy roads. You use a pump to put air into the tire.

A unicycle has one wheel. It's fun to ride!

→ Go to page 22 for activities.

Cars, Planes, Trains

Cars, planes, and trains all have wheels. They have an engine, too. The engine makes the wheels turn fast.

How many wheels does a car have? It has four wheels. It has a steering wheel, too. You turn the steering wheel and the car moves left or right.

A Car

steering wheel

engine

A plane uses wheels to move very fast, and then it flies into the sky. How many wheels can you see?

Trains have metal wheels. The wheels turn on a metal track.

A Train

track

Go to page 23 for activities.

11

5 Wheels for Fun

People use wheels for fun, too! You can see many wheels at the fairground. This big wheel turns, and people go round and round.

A Big Wheel

A Merry-Go-Round

This wheel is a merry-go-round. Children stand on the wheel. Other people push it round and round.

Many toys have wheels. This toy has little wheels. Children sit on it and they use their legs to move.

A Toy

A yo-yo is a wheel. It turns fast and goes up and down.

→ Go to page 24 for activities.

Wheels to Cut

People use wheels to cut things. A round, metal saw is very sharp. The saw uses electricity to turn very fast. It can cut many things. This round saw can cut wood.

A Saw

wood

A Pizza Cutter

Wheels can cut food, too. You can push this cutter on a pizza. The metal wheel turns and it cuts the pizza.

This combine harvester has wheels to move and wheels to cut. The metal wheels are very sharp and they turn fast. The combine harvester moves and the metal wheels cut the wheat.

A Combine Harvester

metal wheels

wheat

Go to page 25 for activities.

Wheels at Home

People use wheels to do many things at home. Look in your home. How many wheels can you find?

This clock has many wheels inside. The wheels turn together, and they make the hands move.

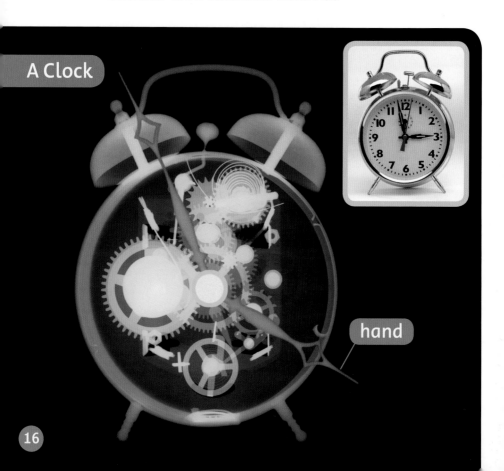

A Clock

hand

A Rolling Pin

This rolling pin is a long wheel. People use a rolling pin to make bread and cookies.

Do you know people can paint with wheels? People use a roller to paint walls.

A Roller

→ Go to page 26 for activities.

 Water and Wind

People use rivers and the wind to turn wheels.

This is an old water mill. The water in the river turns a big wheel. The big wheel turns other wheels in the water mill. The wheels make flour from wheat.

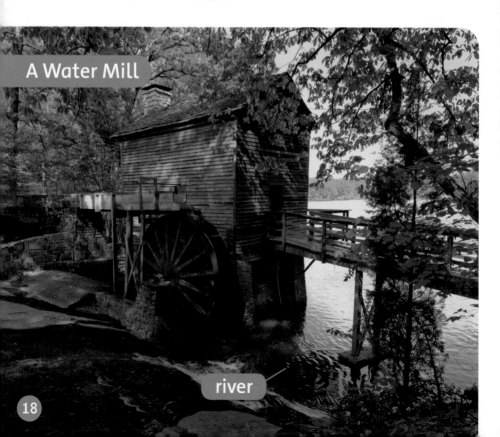

A Water Mill

river

A wind turbine has wheels inside. The wind turns the wheels. This makes electricity.

We use wheels every day, and they help us do many different things. Which is your favorite wheel?

→ Go to page 27 for activities.

19

1 What Are Wheels?

← Read pages 4–5.

1 Write the words.

> roller skates ~~wheelbarrow~~ people bus

1 _wheelbarrow_

2 _____

3 _____

4 _____

2 Complete the sentences.

> little ~~round~~
> big front

1 Wheels are _round_ and they turn.

2 A wheelbarrow has a wheel at the

_____ .

3 A bus has _____ wheels.

4 A roller skate has _____ wheels.

② Carts and Chairs

← Read pages 6–7.

1 Find and write the words.

*pull*strollersportsstorepushwheelchair

1 _____ 2 _____ 3 _____

4 _____ 5 _____ 6 _pull_____

2 Write *true* or *false*.

1 Babies can sleep in strollers.   true

2 A shopping cart has big wheels.   _____

3 People push a shopping cart.   _____

4 People in wheelchairs push the
   wheels with their hands.   _____

3 Bicycles

← Read pages 8–9.

1 Find and write the words.

r	o	t	i	r	e
o	m	e	t	a	l
r	o	a	d	u	d
p	a	p	u	m	p
h	e	l	m	e	t

1 <u>road</u>

2 h

3 p

4 m

5 t

2 Match. Then write the sentences.

You use your legs	to protect your head.
You use a pump	to put air into a tire.
You wear a helmet	to turn bicycle wheels.

1 <u>You use your legs to turn bicycle wheels.</u>

2 _____

3 _____

4 Cars, Planes, Trains

← Read pages 10–11.

1 Write the words.

| car plane train bicycle |

1 _____

2 _____

3 _____

4 _____

2 Write *true* or *false*.

1 A car has six wheels. _____

2 You turn a steering wheel and the car moves left or right. _____

3 Trains don't have wheels. _____

4 Trains move on a metal track. _____

5 Wheels for Fun

← Read pages 12–13.

1 Write the words.

down   left   round   up   right

1 _____
2 _____
3 _____
4 _____
5 _____

2 Complete the sentences.

sit   push   yo-yo   fairground

1 There are many wheels at the _____ .

2 People can _____ a merry-go-round.

3 You can _____ on a toy.

4 A _____ goes up and down.

6 Wheels to Cut

← Read pages 14–15.

1 Match. Then write the sentences.

A combine harvester	cuts wood.
A pizza cutter	cuts wheat.
A saw	cuts pizza.

1 _____

2 _____

3 _____

2 Circle the correct words.

1 A metal saw is very **sharp** / **wood**.

2 A saw turns very **fast** / **food**.

3 A pizza cutter has a metal **wheel** / **pizza**.

4 A combine harvester has wheels to move and wheels to **cutter** / **cut**.

5 A combine harvester **sits** / **moves** and the wheels cut the wheat.

(7) Wheels at Home

← Read pages 16–17.

1 Write the words. Then match.

1 kccol

clock

2 lrlroe

_____

3 lironlgipn

_____

2 Complete the sentences.

long   make   turn   paint

1 People use a rolling pin to _____ bread and cookies.

2 A clock has many wheels that _____ together.

3 People use a roller to _____ walls.

4 A rolling pin is a _____ wheel.

8 Water and Wind

← Read pages 18–19.

electricity   wind turbine
river   water mill

1 Write the words.

1 _____

2 _____

3 _____

4 _____

2 Write *true* or *false*.

1 The wind turns a wheel in a water mill. _____

2 Wheels in a water mill can make flour from wheat. _____

3 The wind turns a wind turbine and this makes electricity. _____

4 You can't use wheels to make electricity. _____

My Wheels

1 Find or draw pictures of wheels. Then write.

Where is it? _____

Is it big or little? _____

Is it fast? _____

Where is it? _____

Is it big or little? _____

Is it fast? _____

Where is it? _____

Is it big or little? _____

Is it fast? _____

Where is it? _____

Is it big or little? _____

Is it fast? _____

2 How many wheels does it have?
Write words.

1 wheel

yo-yo

2 or 3 wheels

4 wheels

many wheels

Picture Dictionary

 air

 bumpy

 children

 cut

 down

 electricity

 fairground

 fast

 flour

 food

 front

 hour

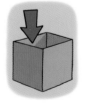 inside

 left

 machine

 metal

 paint

 people

 protect

 pull

 push

 race

 right

 road

 sharp

 sleep

 sports

 store

 turn

 up

 water

 wheel

Oxford Read and Discover

Series Editor: Hazel Geatches • CLIL Adviser: John Clegg

Oxford Read and Discover graded readers are at six levels, for students from age 6 and older. They cover many topics within three subject areas, and support English across the curriculum, or Content and Language Integrated Learning (CLIL).

Available for each reader:
• Audio CD Pack (book & audio CD)
• Activity Book

Teaching notes & CLIL guidance: **www.oup.com/elt/teacher/readanddiscover**

Subject Area / Level	The World of Science & Technology	The Natural World	The World of Arts & Social Studies
1 — 300 headwords	• Eyes • Fruit • Trees • Wheels	• At the Beach • In the Sky • Wild Cats • Young Animals	• Art • Schools
2 — 450 headwords	• Electricity • Plastic • Sunny and Rainy • Your Body	• Camouflage • Earth • Farms • In the Mountains	• Cities • Jobs
3 — 600 headwords	• How We Make Products • Sound and Music • Super Structures • Your Five Senses	• Amazing Minibeasts • Animals in the Air • Life in Rainforests • Wonderful Water	• Festivals Around the World • Free Time Around the World
4 — 750 headwords	• All About Plants • How to Stay Healthy • Machines Then and Now • Why We Recycle	• All About Desert Life • All About Ocean Life • Animals at Night • Incredible Earth	• Animals in Art • Wonders of the Past
5 — 900 headwords	• Materials to Products • Medicine Then and Now • Transportation Then and Now • Wild Weather	• All About Islands • Animal Life Cycles • Exploring Our World • Great Migrations	• Homes Around the World • Our World in Art
6 — 1,050 headwords	• Cells and Microbes • Clothes Then and Now • Incredible Energy • Your Amazing Body	• All About Space • Caring for Our Planet • Earth Then and Now • Wonderful Ecosystems	• Food Around the World • Helping Around the World